HOW DOES A CUT HEAL?

BY ISAAC ASIMOV AND CARRIE DIERKS

Gareth Stevens Publishing
MILWAUKEE

For a free color catalog describing Gareth Stevens's list of high-quality children's books, call 1-800-341-3569 (USA) or 1-800-461-9120 (Canada).

The editor would like to thank Daniel Szeflinski, Jr., and Mark Garnaas for their invaluable assistance regarding the accuracy of this publication.

The book designer would like to thank the models for their participation.

Library of Congress Cataloging-in-Publication Data

Asimov, Isaac, 1920-
    How does a cut heal? / by Isaac Asimov and Carrie Dierks.
      p. cm. -- (Ask Isaac Asimov)
    Includes bibliographical references and index.
    Summary: Describes what happens when the body is cut or bruised, how the body reacts to these injuries, and steps to help the healing process.
    ISBN 0-8368-0805-3
    1. Wound healing--Juvenile literature. [1. Wound healing.
2. Wounds and injuries.] I. Dierks, Carrie. II. Title.
III. Series: Asimov, Isaac, 1920- Ask Isaac Asimov.
RD94.A83   1993   93-18271
617.1'43--dc20

Am. Med. $11.95

Edited, designed, and produced by
Gareth Stevens Publishing
1555 North RiverCenter Drive, Suite 201
Milwaukee, Wisconsin 53212, USA

Text © 1993 by Nightfall, Inc. and Martin H. Greenberg
End matter © 1993 by Gareth Stevens, Inc.
Format © 1993 by Gareth Stevens, Inc.

Picture Credits
pp. 2-3, © Science VU/Visuals Unlimited; pp. 4-5, © Richard T. Nowitz/Picture Perfect USA; pp. 6-7, © Science VU/Visuals Unlimited; p. 6 (inset), © David M. Phillips/Visuals Unlimited; pp. 8-9, © Rudy Lewis/Barnaby's Picture Library; p. 9 (inset), © Bill Beatty/Visuals Unlimited; pp. 10-11, Kurt Carloni/Artisan, 1993; pp. 12-13, © Jon Allyn, Cr. Photog., 1993; pp. 14-15, © Jon Allyn, Cr. Photog., 1993; pp. 16-17, © S. T. Myhill/Barnaby's Picture Library; pp. 18-19, Paul Miller/Advertising Art Studios, 1993; pp. 20-21, © Barnaby's Picture Library; pp. 22-23, © G. Cozzi/K & B News Foto; p. 24, © G. Cozzi/K & B News Foto

Cover photograph, © D. Logan/H. Armstrong Roberts: A deep cut needs stitches in order to heal properly.

Series editor: Barbara J. Behm
Series designer: Sabine Beaupré
Book designer: Kristi Ludwig
Art coordinator: Karen Knutson
Picture researcher: Diane Laska

Printed in the United States of America

1 2 3 4 5 6 7 8 9 98 97 96 95 94 93

Contents

Words that appear in the glossary are printed in **boldface** type the first time they occur in the text.

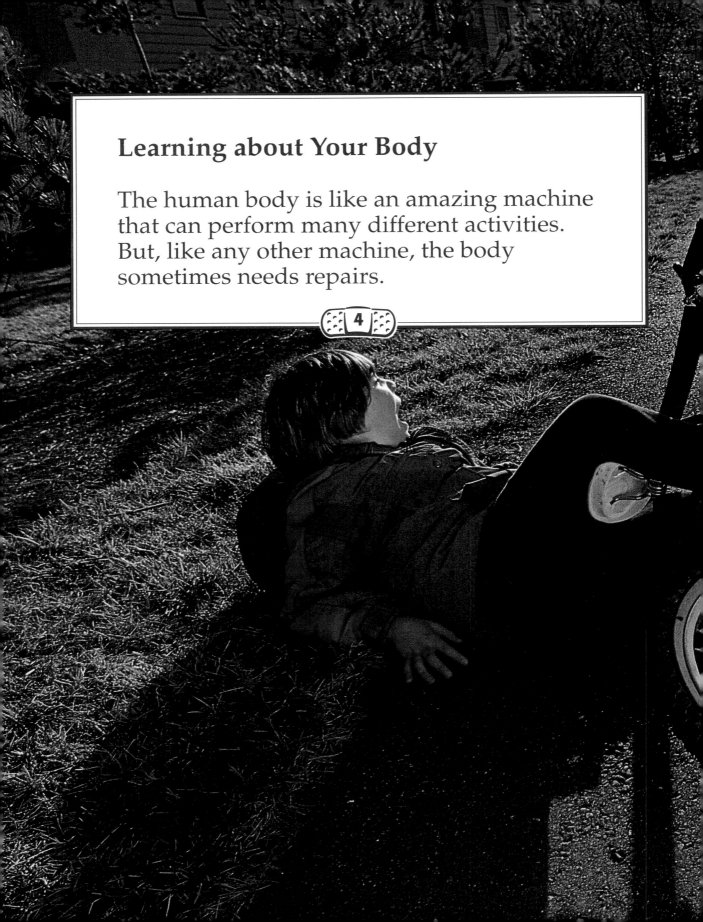

Learning about Your Body

The human body is like an amazing machine that can perform many different activities. But, like any other machine, the body sometimes needs repairs.

4

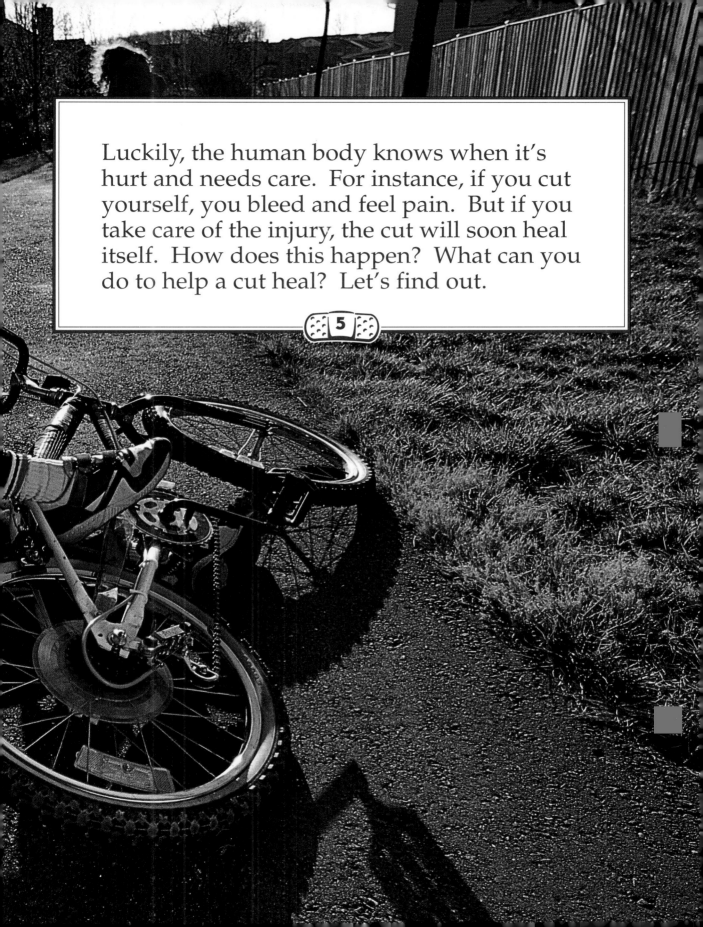

Luckily, the human body knows when it's hurt and needs care. For instance, if you cut yourself, you bleed and feel pain. But if you take care of the injury, the cut will soon heal itself. How does this happen? What can you do to help a cut heal? Let's find out.

5

Life's Precious Liquid

Every moment you are alive, your heart pumps blood to each part of your body. The dark red liquid carries oxygen and nutrients throughout your body, removes wastes, fights disease, and helps keep your body temperature steady.

How does blood travel through your body? Blood vessels called **arteries** carry blood away from the heart, while **veins** return blood to the heart. Tiny **capillaries** connect arteries to veins.

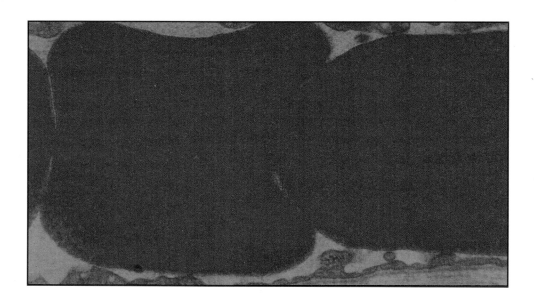

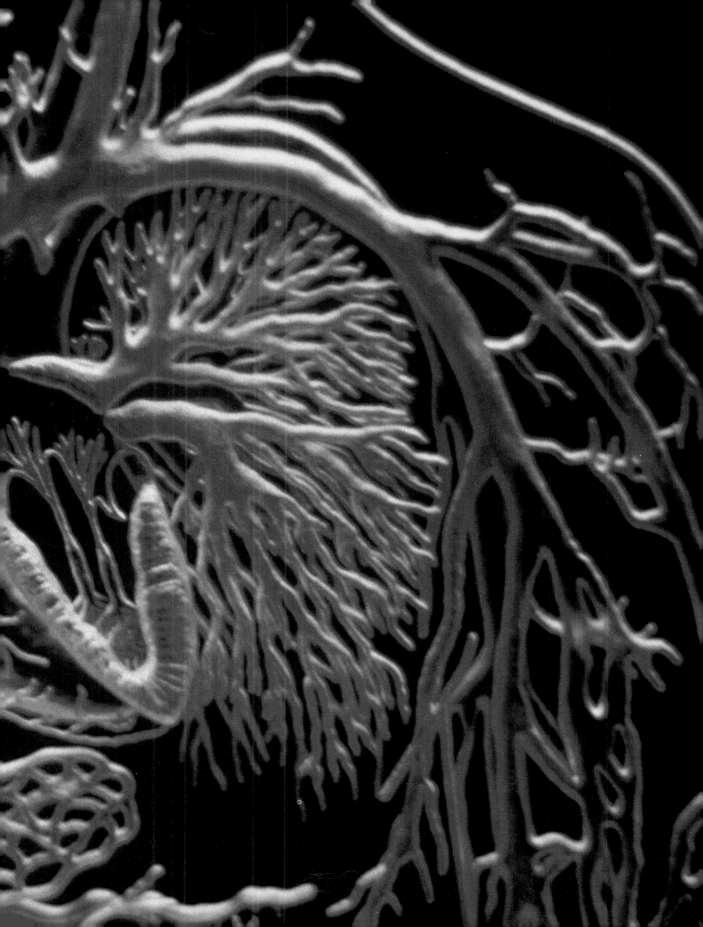

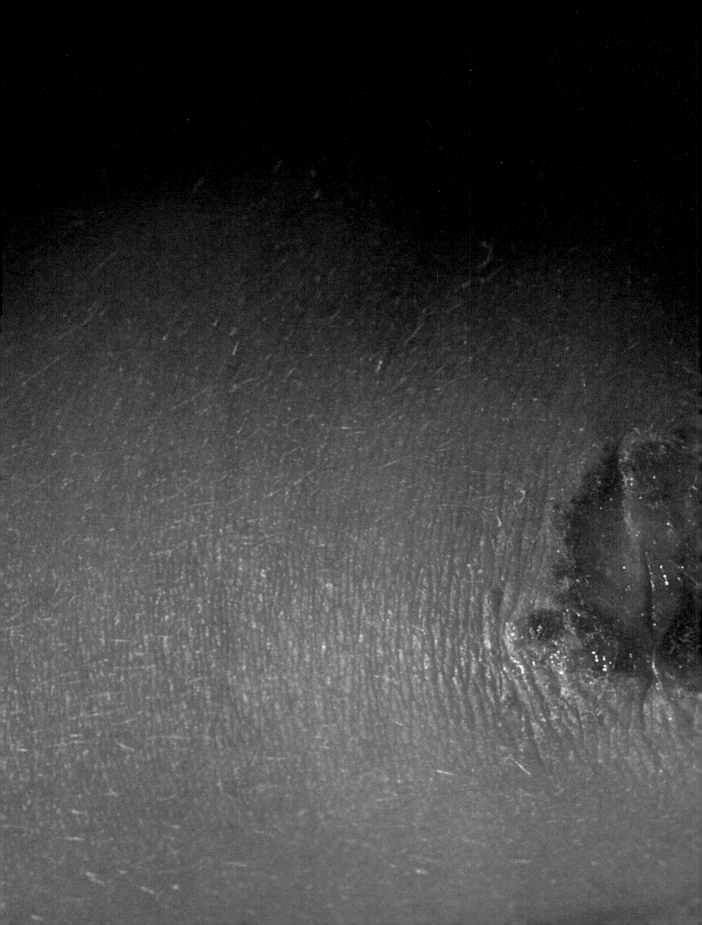

Your Protective Skin

Capillaries are located just below the surface of the skin. So even a mild bump or scrape will probably break some of the numerous capillaries. This will form a bruise.

If the skin breaks open, you will bleed. But a cut causes more than a loss of blood. It also forms an opening where disease-causing **bacteria** can enter your bloodstream. For these reasons, it is important to stop the bleeding and help the broken skin heal.

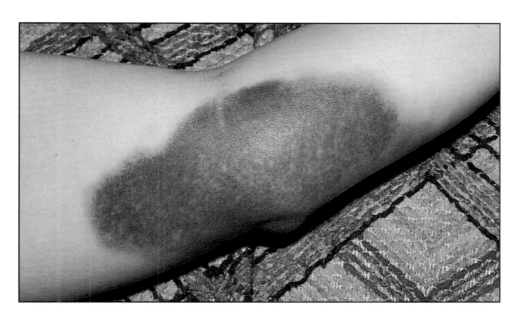

A Built-In Plug

How does bleeding stop? When you cut yourself, tiny disk-shaped structures in the blood called **platelets** gather at the wound. The platelets react with chemicals in the blood, creating a mesh of sticky fibers, or fibrin. These fibers cover the wound, create a clot, and block the flow of blood.

People whose blood does not form these fibers have a disease called **hemophilia**. They must try not to hurt themselves.

10

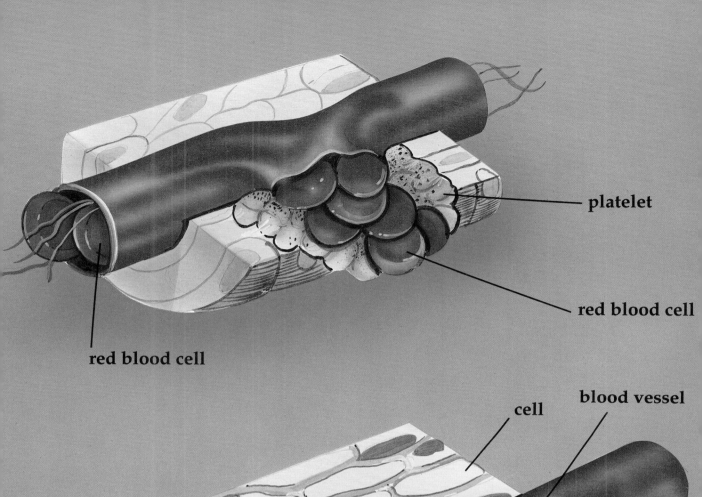

platelet

red blood cell

red blood cell

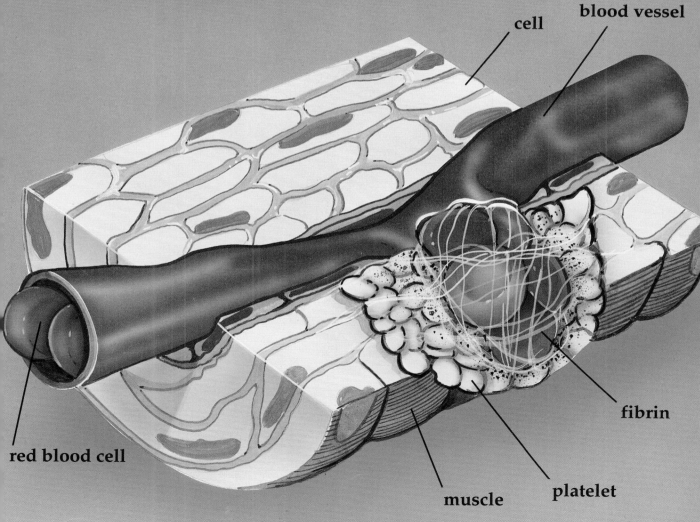

cell

blood vessel

fibrin

red blood cell

muscle

platelet

Leave the Cut Alone!

Eventually, the dried blood over the wound hardens into a crusty **scab**. The scab protects the skin and blood vessels while they repair themselves. What happens if you scratch open a scab before the cut is completely healed? That's right — the cut will open, and you will start to bleed again. But if you leave the area alone, the cut will heal. Then the scab will eventually loosen and fall off by itself.

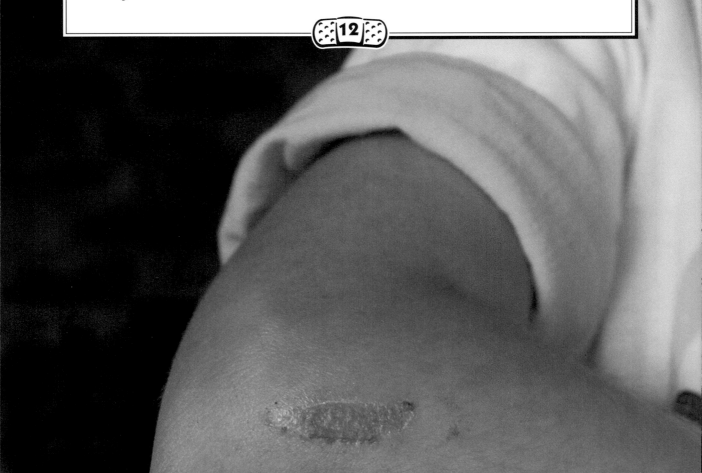

White Blood Cells to the Rescue

Sometimes a cut becomes red, swollen, and warm to the touch. These are signs that your body is fighting an **infection**. An infection occurs because harmful bacteria have entered the bloodstream.

At the first sign of infection, thousands of **white blood cells** surround and kill the bacteria. Later, the cut will release a substance called **pus**, a yellowish liquid that contains dead bacteria and white blood cells.

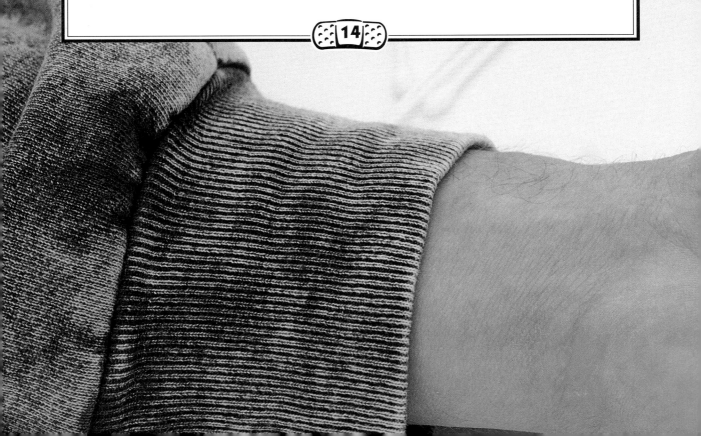

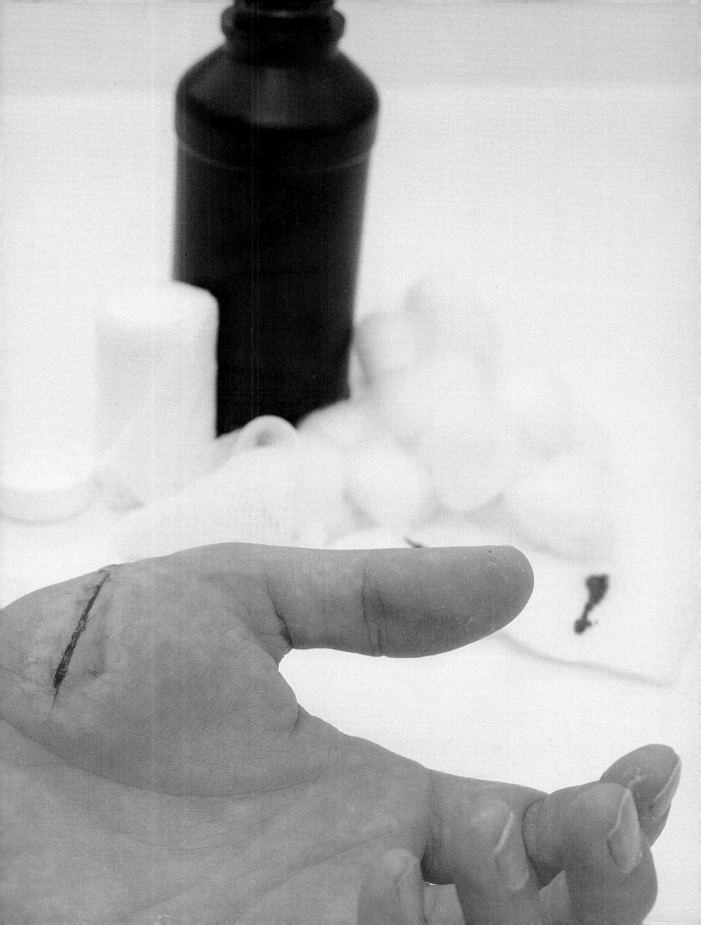

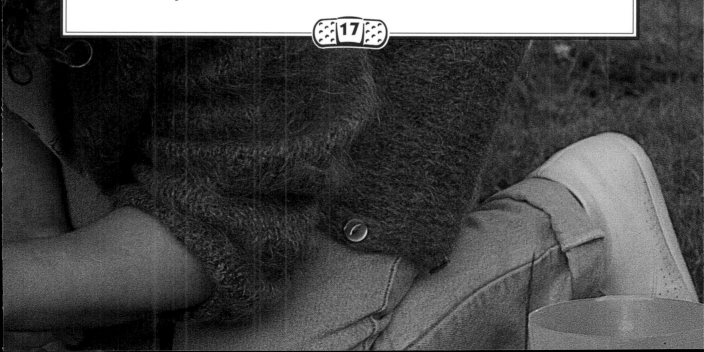

First Aid for Minor Cuts

Your body has a remarkable ability to repair itself. But there are certain things you can do to help a cut heal. Most small cuts will stop bleeding by themselves. But if a cut doesn't stop bleeding right away, press firmly on the wound with a clean cloth or gauze.

Once the bleeding has stopped, wash the area with mild soap. Then, put a bandage on the wound. A bandage not only keeps the cut from opening again, it also keeps out dirt and bacteria. It is a good idea to keep a first-aid kit handy to take care of the cuts and scrapes that happen so often. The kit will allow you to take immediate action.

EMERGENCY!

A deep cut that breaks a vein or artery needs fast, professional medical care. CALL FOR HELP IMMEDIATELY! Before this care arrives, the injured person should lie down and raise the injured area. Press directly on the wound with a clean cloth or gauze. Do not remove this cloth. Add another cloth on top if the first one bleeds through. If the bleeding continues, apply pressure to the artery that is carrying blood to the wound. These areas are called **pressure points**.

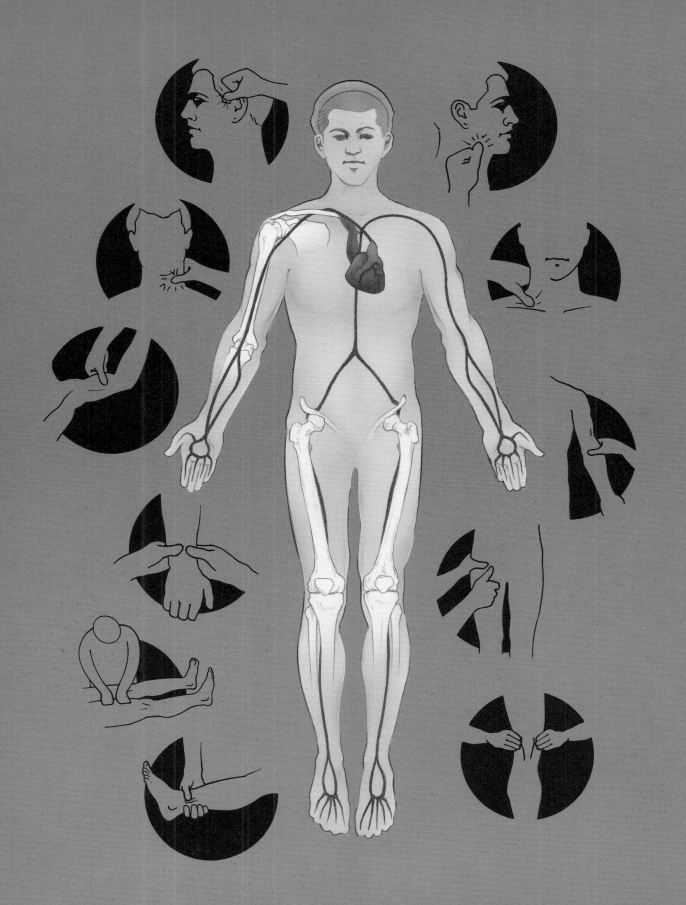

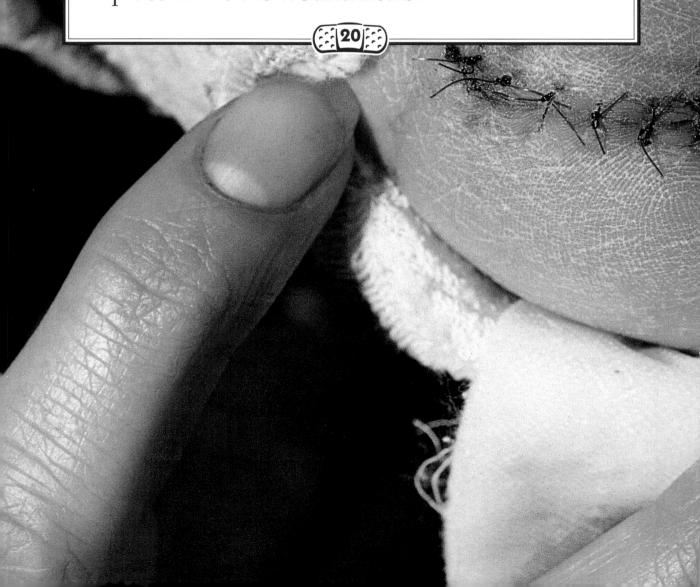

A Stitch in Time

A large or deep cut needs a doctor's care to heal properly. First, the doctor carefully cleans the wound. Then she or he stitches the wound together with a special needle and thread. The stitches hold the **tissues** in place while the wound heals.

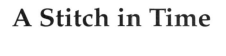

20

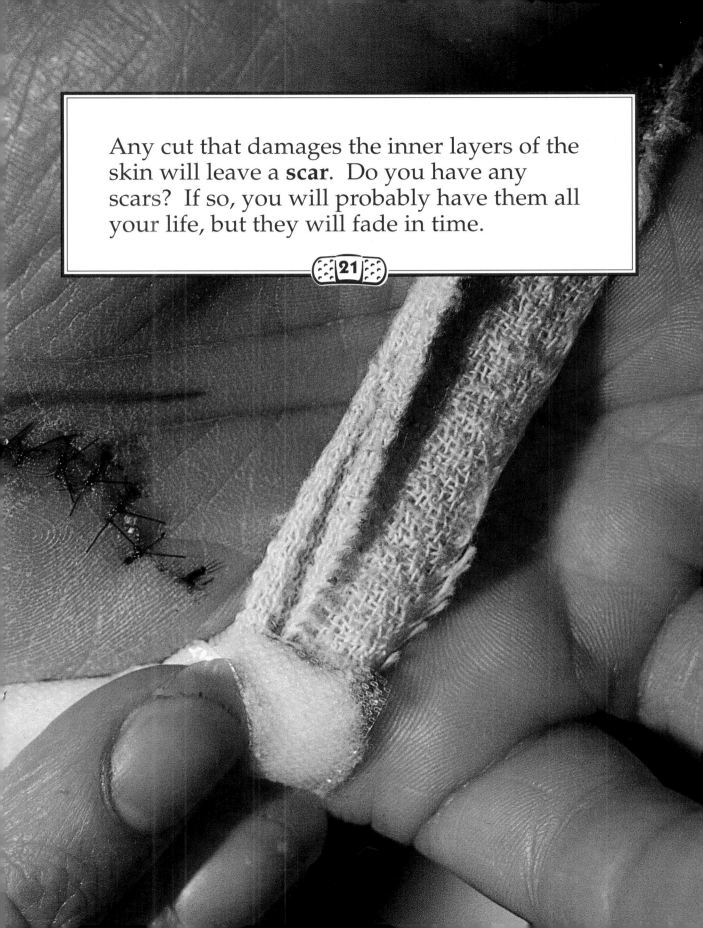

Any cut that damages the inner layers of the skin will leave a **scar**. Do you have any scars? If so, you will probably have them all your life, but they will fade in time.

21

Amazing Healing Powers

It's never fun to get a cut. But the next time you fall off your bike, you'll see the body's amazing healing powers at work. If the wound is minor, just keep it clean and protected — your body will do the rest!

22

More Books to Read

A Drop of Blood by Paul Showers (Crowell)
The Emergency Book: You Can Save a Life! by Bradley Smith and Gus
    Stevens (Simon & Schuster)
Your Heart and Blood by Leslie Jean Le Master (Childrens Press)

Places to Write

Here are some places you can write for more information about
first aid. Be sure to state exactly what you want to know. Give
them your full name and address so they can write back to you.

American Red Cross
17th and D Streets, N.W.
Washington, D.C. 20006

Canadian Red Cross Society
1800 Alta Vista Drive
Ottawa, Ontario
K1G 4J5

Glossary

arteries (ARE-ter-eez): vessels that carry blood from the heart to
    the rest of the body.

bacteria (back-TEER-ih-uh): one-celled organisms, invisible to the
    human eye, that live almost everywhere. Some bacteria are
    harmful to humans.

capillaries (CAP-ih-lare-eez): tiny blood vessels that connect veins
    and arteries.

hemophilia (heem-oh-FILL-ih-uh): a blood disorder in which a
    wound does not stop bleeding properly.

infection (in-FECK-shun): a condition that occurs in the body
    when harmful types of bacteria or other harmful organisms
    invade it.

platelets (PLATE-lets): structures in the blood that help stop a
   wound from bleeding.

pressure points (PRESH-ur poynts): places on the body where
   blood vessels run near a bone. These points can be compressed
   to slow down the flow of blood.

pus: a yellowish liquid that contains dead bacteria and white
   blood cells.

scab: dried blood and other fluids that form a hard crust over
   a wound.

scar: a mark left on the skin after a wound heals.

tissues (TISH-ooze): collections of cells of a certain type.

veins (vanes): vessels that return blood to the heart from another
   part of the body.

white blood cells: structures in the blood that kill bacteria and
   other foreign bodies.

Index